Seahorses

Judy Wearing

Published by Weigl Publishers Inc.
350 5th Avenue, Suite 3304, PMB 6G
New York, NY 10118-0069
Website: www.weigl.com

Library of Congress Cataloging-in-Publication Data

Wearing, Judy.
 Seahorses / Judy Wearing.
     p. cm. -- (World of wonder)
 Includes index.
 ISBN 978-1-60596-102-6 (hard cover : alk. paper) -- ISBN 978-1-60596-103-3 (soft cover : alk. paper)
 1. Sea horses--Juvenile literature. I. Title.
 QL638.S9W42 2010
 597'.6798--dc22
                           2009004986

Printed in China
1 2 3 4 5 6 7 8 9 0 13 12 11 10 09

Editor: Heather C. Hudak
Design and Layout: Terry Paulhus

Weigl acknowledges Getty Images as its primary image supplier for this title.

CONTENTS

What is a Seahorse?

Have you ever seen a fish that reminds you of a farm animal? This may have been a seahorse. A seahorse is a kind of fish. It has a long, slender body with a curled tail.

There are about 35 kinds of seahorses. They live in **coral** reefs or **sea grass** near the ocean shore.

Can you guess why these fish are called seahorses? Look at the shape of their head.

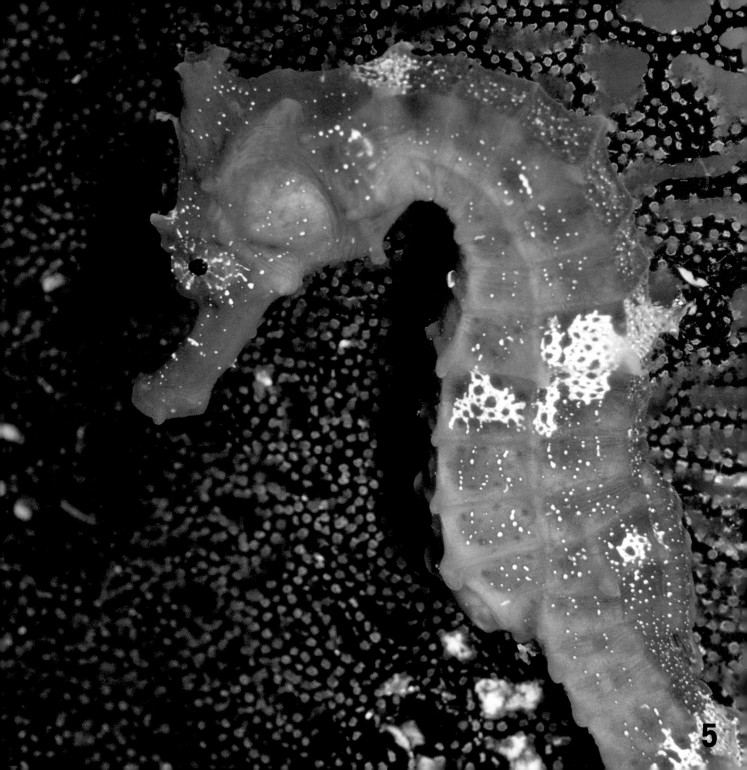

5

Seahorse Size

Did you know that the smallest seahorses are about the size of a quarter? One of the smallest seahorses is the dwarf seahorse. It grows up to 2 inches (5 centimeters) long. One of the largest seahorses is the big-bellied seahorse. It is almost as long as a ruler.

Seahorse Skin

No two seahorses look the same. The pattern of bumps and spines on their head is special to each seahorse.

Most types of fish have smooth **scales**. Instead, seahorses have skin stretched over small plates of bone. This makes them look bumpy.

A seahorse's bony plates can be very tough or prickly. For this reason, some birds and crabs will not eat seahorses.

9

Moving Forward

Did you know that seahorses do not have ears? If you look closely, you will see flaps on the sides of their head where ears would be. These are very small fins. They help **steer** the seahorse through water.

Seahorses have another small fin on their back. To swim, they quickly wave this fin back and forth.

Seahorses are slow swimmers. They move fastest when they push their belly against the water. They do this the same way you push your body forward when skating.

11

Straw Snout

How do seahorses eat? Seahorses have no teeth. They use their mouth like a straw to suck up food.

The mouth of a seahorse is long and thin. The top and bottom **jaws** are joined to make a tube. They use the tube to suck up **shrimp** or other small animals that swim nearby.

Seahorses can move each eye in a different direction. This helps them search larger areas for food.

All Wrapped Up

What do seahorses have in common with monkeys? They can use their tail to grasp objects.

Seahorses often wrap their tail around plants or coral. This keeps them from floating away in moving waters.

15

Can You Spot the Seahorse?

Have you ever seen a seahorse in nature? Seahorses often blend in with their **habitat**. They change color to match the rocks or plants around them. They also grow bumps or flaps on their skin to look like coral.

Seahorses spend a great deal of time staying still. They hide in the sea grass or coral. When they move, seahorses swim slowly.

Super Dads

Did you know that male seahorses carry the babies? The female puts her eggs inside a **pouch** on the male's belly. Most seahorses have between 100 and 200 eggs in their pouch at a time.

The male takes care of the eggs in his belly for about two to four weeks. The day the babies are born, they swim away to look after themselves. Later that same day, the female comes and gives the male more eggs.

Saving Seahorses

Did you know that there are only half as many seahorses in the oceans as there once were? There are ways to help keep seahorses from becoming **extinct**.

Each year, 20 million seahorses are used to make **medicine**. People think it will make them feel well. Other people take seahorses from the ocean to keep in fish tanks as pets. One way to help keep seahorses safe is to stop using them in medicine or keeping them as pets.

Seahorse Hide and Seek

Supplies

two sheets of red construction paper, one sheet of yellow construction paper, scissors, and a timer

1. With the help of an adult, cut out 12 seahorse shapes from one sheet of red construction paper. Then, cut 12 little seahorse shapes from one sheet of yellow construction paper.

2. Place the yellow seahorses on the uncut piece of red construction paper. Set the timer for one minute.

3. Pretend you are a crab. Crabs eat seahorses. How many can you pick up in one minute?

4. Then, place the red seahorses on the piece of red construction paper. Set the timer for one minute.

5. How many red seahorses can you pick up in one minute?

6. Did you pick up more red seahorses or yellow seahorses? Is it easier to see seahorses when they are the same color as their surroundings or a different color?

7. How does being the same color as their habitat help seahorses escape their enemies?

Find Out More

To learn more about seahorses, visit these websites.

Shedd Aquarium
www.sheddaquarium.org/
SEA/seahorse/index.html

BillyBear4Kids.Com
www.billybear4kids.com/
animal/whose-toes/
toes25a.html

Seahorse World, Australia
www.seahorseworld.com.au

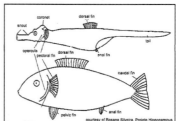

Project Seahorse
http://seahorse.fisheries.
ubc.ca/faq.html

Glossary

coral: a hard, stony substance in the ocean that is made by a soft animal

extinct: no longer living any place on Earth

habitat: the place where an animal lives in nature

jaws: the upper and lower bones surrounding the mouth

medicine: a substance that is used to help sick people get better

pouch: a part of the body that is like a pocket

scales: small, flat plates that overlap on the surface of fish or reptiles

sea grass: a grass-like plant that grows on the ocean floor

shrimp: animals that live in water and have a hard shell, many legs, and feelers

steer: guide the direction something moves

Index